GLICS ;)

* T. L. Meadows *

Microcontent

GLICS ;)

(Geek Lingo Internet & Communication Savvy)

Who I am:

Certified Geek, Elancer, Net Head, Techie, Technocowboy, Web Hippie and Guru etc... etc... etc... attempting to Webify Newbies and Denizens by offering simple tutorials, and other avenues to help the user, both young and old, become more **Geek Lingo Internet and Communication Savvy.**
Bla, bla, bla...

Let's just get to the core and I'll tell you

What This Book Is About:

This handbook is a reference tool so that you may quickly upgrade to a Netizen by deciphering the codes used to communicate within the Cyber world and thus lead you down the road to becoming a noticeable Cytizen <-- don't worry there is also a word list at the back of this book!

Have you ever been in a chat room on the Internet or received a text message on your cell phone that looked like it was from another planet, or perhaps it left you believing that you had forgotten how to read, or maybe, just maybe, there may be something wrong with your eyes? Oh, never mind, here is an example of this Technobabble --> **GTSY ;)**

This book will also <u>attempt</u> to teach you some Netiquette like the

#1 rule --> **Don't be an (_|_)**

Whether your familiar with this jargon or not this **ISS** aid will help you to Encode and Decode Geek Lingo and come to terms with some of the terms <-- this makes your Cyber life more comfortable as well as the rest of the Cytizens -->

Meaning:
ITIA
TEOTWAWKI

GET WITH IT! B^)

Netiquette
:) (:

Network + Etiquette:

The code of conduct that people are expected to <-- should --> follow while communicating via the net. Although there are no official rules, the set of rules here <-- if broken --> can get you kicked out of a various forums or be ditzed by other Netizens.

So here's the

RAW:

* Respect Others --> Don't be an (_|_)
* Don't Give TMI to Strangers
* No SHOUTING
* No Spamming
* No Mouse Trapping
* Don't Feed The Trolls
* 2 Flame is 2B Flamed <-- Try not 2B an MP
* 2B Ignored is 2 Ignore
* C Topic <-- follow --> and know when 2 *poof*
* +1=X sessions can byte :-D"" on the (_|_)
* Get 2 the Point <-- DWAN

In case your worried ^--> by the time you finish the book this should All make some sense!

Emoticons

;)

Pronounced: e-moh-tih-cons

Oddball keyboard characters used to express one's self in a chat room, e-mail, or text messaging. To put it another way they are ASCII characters that represent emotion. In other words --> an emoticon tells someone what you really mean without having to explain your feelings.

Look at this emoticon -->   **:-)**   <-- it is a simple Smiley that lies on it side <-- which the majority do! Now imagine that the colon is the eyes, the dash is the nose, and the right parenthesis is the mouth <--Get it? I cannot explain it any better than that!

In the two-dimensional cyber world emoticons grew out of the need to display feelings <-- for example --> when you speak to someone face to face we use facial expressions to convey what we mean, thus, emoticons are the nets equivalent to this. This chapter will expose you to these characters and give you their meaning.

Mind you that although this list is extensive it probably will not have every single emoticon out there but it will <u>attempt</u> to give you the most widely known <-- who knows how many have been created and caught on as you explore this guide! Maybe, just maybe, this will give you ideas to create your own and you will see it in the next GLICS handbook **;-)**

Be Forewarned --> Any neck strains, or injuries incurred from tilting of the head sideways I will not be held responsible! <-- However, some emoticons don't require you to tilt your head to see them.

The emoticons are in the following

Categories:
Smileys, Pets, BMOC, Straights, and Items

So read on and

<u>Get Upgraded!</u> **B^)**

Smileys
:)

The Basics:

:)	<-- Little Smiley		:-)	<-- Big Smiley
;)	<-- Little Winky		;-)	<-- Big Winky
:D	<-- Little Laugh		:-D	<-- Big Laugh
:(	<-- Little frown		:-(	<-- Big Frown

Intense Basics:

:~-(	<-- Bawling		:-X..	<-- Big Wet Kiss
;-(	<-- Chin up		:-S	<-- Confused
:-@!	<-- Cursing		:-e	<-- Disappointed
:")	<-- Embarrassed		>-)	<-- Evil Grin
8-)	<-- Excited		|-{	<-- Good Grief
:-|	<-- Grim		8-|	<-- In Suspense
>;->	<-- Lewd Remark		X-(	<-- Mad
&-1	<-- Makes Me Cry		:-S	<-- Makes No Sense
:I	<-- Not amusing		8-O	<-- Oh My God!
:-t	<-- Pouting		:-C	<-- Real Unhappy
:-O	<-- Shocked		;^}	<-- Smirking

8-]   <-- Wow Man   :-(O)   <-- Yelling

|-O   <-- Yawning   =8-O   <-- Yikes!

On The Wild Side:

%-6   <-- Brain Dead   :*)   <-- Drinking Every Night

:#)   <-- Drunk   %-D   <-- Drunk & Laughing

:-$ <-- Feeling Sick   ?-(<-- Has a Black Eye

*%-(<-- Hung-over

*@%-(<-- Hung-over with a Headache

%-)   <-- Partying

#-)   <-- Partied All Night Long

Lip Service:

:-D""   <-- Blabber Mouth   :-(=) <-- Bucktoothed

:-)... <-- Drooling   :-6   <-- Eating Spices

:-!   <-- Foot In Mouth   :-W <-- Forked Tongue

:oP   <-- Grin W/Tongue Out   :-X <-- Kiss Kiss

:-9   <-- Licking Lips   :-# <-- Lips Are Sealed

:-{} <-- Lipstick   :-{) <-- Moustache

:-*   <-- OOPS!   :-"   <-- Puckered Lips

:-i   <-- Smoking a Cig   :-?   <-- Smoking a Pipe

:-Q <-- Smoking & Talking   :-P <-- Tongue Out

:-& <-- Tongue Tied   :-a <-- Tongue to Nose

:-" <-- Whistling |-P <-- Yuck!

Mop Heads:

(:-) <-- Bald Headed   d:-) <-- Baseball Cap

q:-) <-- Baseball Cap Backwards   /:-) <-- Beret Hat

&:-) <-- Curly Hair   <:-1 <-- Dunce Hat

#:-) <-- Hair is a Mess   {:-) <-- Hair Parted

X:-) <-- Propeller Head   ~:-) <-- Single Hair

B:-) <-- Shades on Head   @:-) <-- Wavy Hair

{(:-) <-- Toupee   [:-) <-- Walkman

OddBalls:

:-}X <-- Bow Tie-Wearing   H-) <-- Cross-Eyed

:O   <-- Hungry   :^) <-- Got Personality

B^) <-- Geeky --> With Horn-Rimmed Glasses

+-(<-- Hit Between the Eyes |-(<-- Lost Glasses

:-(<| <-- Standing Firm |:-) <-- UniBrow

8^) <-- Wearing Shades

Downloading... B^)

Pets

3:]

:=8) <-- Baboon   : = <-- Beaver

}:-o <-- Bull   pq}:-o <-- Bull W Body

}{ <-- Butterfly   }~{ <-- Butterfly/prettier

~M`' <-- Camel   Q* <-- Cat

& <-- Cat Cleaning   48> <-- Chicken

3:-o <-- Cow   pp3:-o <-- Cow W/Body

:93-< <-- Dog   .\/ <-- Duck

6\/) <-- Elephant   >--o) <-- Fish

8) <-- Frog   8)~* <-- Frog Caught Fly

8:] <-- Gorilla   ~n` <-- Horse

<:3)~~~~ <-- Mouse   :=) <-- Orangutan

8>-: <-- Penguin   3:] <-- Pet Smiley

:@) <--Pig   ~))))'> <-- Possum

`~~~:[<-- Rattle Snake   ~~~~:} <-- Snake

_@/ <-- Snail   Qb <-- Turtle

48>=: <--Turkey   :<= <-- Walrus

Processing Information... B^)

BMOC

~=#:-) \

Star Gazing:

=|:-)= <-- Abe Lincoln   =|:^0 <-- Bill Clinton

:-.)   <-- Cindy Crawford   Q[:-) <-- Davy Crockett

&:-)-8 <-- Dolly Parton   }:-[<-- Dracula

5:-y <-- Elvis   :^{= <-- Frank Zappa

[I:-I <-- FrankenStein

4:^) <-- George Washington

(_8^(|)   <--Homer Simpson

@@@@:-) <--Marge Simpson

?:^[] <-- Jim Carrey   (8 { <-- John Lennon

>:-1 <-- Klingon   8(:-) <-- Micky Mouse

%\v <-- Picasso   :--^) <--Pinocchio

+0:-) <-- Pope   7:^] <--President Reagan

([(<-- Robocop   !~? <-- Rocky

3:*> <-- Rudolph   *<|:-)} <-- Santa Claus

-(:)(0)=8 <-- Teletubby   =):^) <-- Uncle Sam

B-)==> <-- ZZ Top

Story Time:

O:-) <-- Angel   **>:-E** <-- Bucktoothed Vampire

>:-F <--Bucktoothed Vampire with One Tooth Missing

\o/ <-- Cheerleader   **8=:-)** <-- Chef

*<):o) <-- Clown   **c):-)** <-- Cowboy

@-) <-- Cyclops   **]:->** <-- Demon

>:-> <-- Devil   **>:)** <-- Little Devil

<:-l <-- Dunce   **=:-H** <-- Football player

Q:-) <-- Graduate   **o[-<]:** <-- Skater

+<||-) <-- Knight   **8:-)** <-- Little Girl

k:-) <-- Little Boy W/Propeller

:-) :- <-- Man   **:-)8 :** <-- Woman

):-(<-- Nordic   **+<:-)** <-- Nun

P-(<-- Pirate   **!~[** <-- Prizefighter

=:-) <-- Punk   **--:-)** <-- Punk W/ Mohawk

(((((:-{= <-- Rave Dude   **[:]** <-- Robot

[:|] <-- Big Robot   **0>-</** <--Snowboarder

>:-[<-- Vampire   **<]:^}** <-- Witch

~=#:-) <-- Wizard   **~=#:-) ** <-- With Wand

Still Processing... B^)

Straights

('6,')

Straight-On's:

}|{   <-- Butterfly   })i({ <-- Butterfly/Prettier

>^,,^< <-- Kitty Cat   /(-'.'-)\ <-- Puppy dog

@(*0*)@ <-- Koala   ('6,')   <-- Smiley

From the Side:

.'J <--Smiley   .'r <-- Tongue Sticking Out

.'v <-- Talking   .'T <-- Neutral

.'y <-- Whistling   .'\ <-- Frowning

.^J <--Smiley W/Pointy Nose .'V <-- Yelling

.'U <-- Yawning   .'s <-- Lipstick

Assicons:

(_|_) <-- Ass

(_o_) <-- Ass Thats Been Around(_O_) <-- And More...

(Y) <-- Butt   (_^_) <-- Bubble Butt

(Y) <-- Big Butt   (_?_) <-- Dumb Ass

(_._) <-- Flat Ass   (_#_) <-- Got Ass Pounding

(_X_) <-- Get Off My Ass (_x_) <-- Kiss My Ass

(__!__) <-- Large Ass   (_!__) <-- Lopsided Ass

(_$_) <-- Money Coming Out of his Ass

(_!_) <-- Nice Ass   (_E=3Dmc2_) <-- Smart Ass

(_*_) <--Sore Loser   {_!_} <-- Squishy Ass

(!)   <-- Tight Ass   (_zzz_) <-- Tired Ass

(_o^o_) <-- Wise Ass   (_13_) <--Unlucky Ass

(_x_)   <-- Kissing Ass Goodbye
**

Boobiecons:

o o   <-- A cup   [_] [_] <-- Alien

|oo| <-- Android   (O)(O) <-- Big

(o Y o) <-- Boobiecons   {.}{.}   <-- Cold

(.Y.)   <-- Curvy   { O }{ O } <-- D cup

(,) (,) <-- Droopy   ($)($) <-- Expensive Fakes

\o/\o/ <-- Grandma   (+)(+) <-- Fakes

(. Y .) <-- Fat   .Y.   <-- Flat

(^)(^) <-- Freezing   (*)(*)   <-- High Eyes

(@) (@) <--Large Eyes   (.)(.)   <-- IBTC

(o)(O) <-- Lopsided   (') (') <-- Perky

(Q)(Q) <-- Pierced   (o)(o)   <-- Regular

(p)(p) <-- Tassled Pasties   (oYo) <-- Wonder Bra

Items

~O-O~

(:::::[]:::::) <--- Band Aid

|o---| <-- In Bed

(_)3 <-- Beer Mug

<----D <-- Bow & Arrow

_/7 <-- Cup

\%/ <-- Drink

<;;;;=0 <-- Knife

O~~~O <-- Handcuffs

(_() <-- Marshmallow

<%) <-- Pizza

@>}-`-,- <-- Rose

~O-O~ <-- (Sun)Glasses

==--- <-- Toothbrush

(#) <-- Waffle

|=---| <-- Bed

(|X0||) <-- Big Mac

::::::[]:::::: <-- Belt

[{------]}> <--Crayon

[>O <-- Diamond Ring

3--- <-- Fork

(|0|) <-- Hamburger

<3 <-- Heart/Love

0|-) <-- Net Religion

\&&&/ <-- Pretzels

C--- <-- Spoon

<;;;;;;;;;;;|===0 <-- Sword

`~)_)~´ <-- Toilet paper

:) (: <-- Chat

**== <--USA Flag

Download Complete
Whew! B^"

<-- | White Space <-- use it...
   V

Shortys

GTSY!

AKA: Internet Acronyms = E-mail Shorthand

   Gathered from the first letters of a phrase, Shortys are the Internet's equivalent to shorthand <-- which has been used for decades --> like when a boss dictates to a secretary and she/he writes down a bunch of symbols to keep pace with his/her normal speech <-- yep it's kinda just like that!

   In a chat room it can be very tedious for the user when they are typing a long phrase in response to a subject <-- and in the interim others are also responding --> and by the time you have plugged in a response the conversation has already turned to something else, thus, causing someone to back scroll to remember what in the world you were talking about way back when <-- if they decide to and don't become so bored that they eventually leave the room, or don't chat with you, OR close this book --> so let's hurry and move on to the

Bottom Line:

 Communication in the cyber world is extremely fast paced and there are usually dozens <-- and I mean dozens --> of people competing to let their thoughts be known <-- Shortys are a useful tool to deal with all that and let's face it --> Shortys are fun and its really cool to chat in a lingo that a lot of people <-- Denizens --> don't understand --> yet! :)

Also --> the screens on digital phones aren't very big! **LOL** <-- which means --> **L**augh **O**ut **L**oud and this leads us to our

First and Only Lesson:

   Here's another example -->**GTSY** <-- **G**lad **T**o **S**ee **Y**a. The letters that make the word are in **bold**. See **ISS** <-- **I**t's **S**o **S**imple <--Get It? Also some Shortys have numbers like -->**F2F** <-- **F**ace **TO** **F**ace.

Now remember --> Shortys are in **UPPERCASE**, which is perfectly acceptable and not considered shouting. I would also like to add that it used to be a rule that Shortys were only created if they could be pronounced vocally like **GTSY** --> **jit-see** <-- **C**? This is no longer the case <-- although if you create a Sound Shorty you truly have hit a high note! **;)**

BCNU now -->

GO Decode! B^)

A

A/S/L	<-- Age/Sex/Location	ASAP	<-- As Soon As Possible
AATK	<-- Always At Keyboard	ASF	<-- And So Forth
AAMOF	<-- As A Matter Of Fact	ASL	<-- Assistant Section Leader
ABT	<-- AbouT		
ACD	<-- Alt Control Delete	ASOP	<-- Assistant System Operator
AND	<-- Any Day Now		
AFAIK	<-- As Far As I Know	ATM	<-- At The Moment
AFAYC	<-- As Far As Your Concerned	ATSL	<-- Along The Same Line
AFK	<-- Away From Keyboard	ATSX	<-- At The Same Time
AFUP	<-- All F**ked Up	AWA	<-- As Well As
AI	<-- Artificial Intelligence/ As If	AWS	<-- As We Speak
		AWHFY?	<-- Are We Having Fun Yet?
AIAMU	<-- And I'm A Monkey's Uncle		
		AWOL	<-- Absent/Away With Out Leave
AIH	<-- As It Happens		
AIIC	<-- As If I Care	AWYR	<-- Awaiting Your Reply
AISI	<-- As I See It		
AKA	<-- Also Known As	AYOR	<-- At Your Own Risk
ALA	<-- As Long As	AYPI?	<-- And Your Point Is?
ALAP	<-- As Long As Possible	AYS?	<-- Are You Stupid?
AML	<-- All My Love		
AOAS	<-- All Of A Sudden		
AOB	<-- Abuse Of Bandwidth		
AP	<-- Apple Pie :)		

B

B/C	<-- BeCause	BLT	<-- Bacon Lettuce & Tomato ;)
B4	<-- BeFORE		
B4N	<-- Bye FOR Now	BME	<-- Byte ME
BAB	<-- Build A Bridge	BMOC	<-- Big Man On Campus
BAC	<-- Back At Computer	BMTA	<-- Brilliant Minds Think Alike
BAF	<-- Brain Already Fried		
BBL8R	<-- Be Back LATER	BNI	<-- Batteries Not Included
BBS	<-- Bulletin Board System	BOB	<-- Back Off Buddy
		BOC	<-- But Of Course
BCL	<-- Be CooL	BOF	<-- Boring Old Fart
BCNU	<-- Be Seeing You	BOT	<-- Back On Topic
BF	<-- BoyFriend	BOHICA	<-- Bend Over Here It Comes Again
BFD	<-- Big F**king Deal		
BFFL	<-- Best Friends For Life	BOT	<-- Back On Topic
		BRB	<-- BathRoom Break
BGUTI	<-- Better Get Used To It	BS	<-- Bull S**t
		BSOD	<-- Blue Screen Of Death
BHOF	<-- Bald Headed Old Fart	BTOBS	<-- Be There Or Be Square
		BTSOOM	<-- Beats The S**t Out Of Me
BIF	<-- Basic In Fact		
BION	<-- Believe It Or Not	BTW	<-- By The Way
BIOYIOP	<-- Blow It Out Your I/O Port	BUGS	<-- Bad User Generated Symptoms
BITD	<-- Back In The Day	BYOB	<-- Bring Your Own Bottle
BITMT	<-- But In The Mean Time		

C

C4N	<-- Ciao For Now
CAD	<-- Computer Aided Design
CADET	<-- Can't Add-Doesn't Even Try
CATCH	<-- Come Again? That Can't Help
CBL8R	<-- Come Back **Later**
CBT	<-- Computer Based Training
CDIWY	<-- Couldn't Do It Without You
CD-ROM	<-- Consumer Device Rendered Obsolete in Months
CERT	<-- Computer Emergency Response Team
CFY	<-- Calling For You
CIO	<-- Chief Information Officer
CID	<-- Crying In Disgrace/ Consider It Done
CINP	<-- Continue In Next Post
CM@TW	<-- Catch Me AT The Web
CMF	<-- Count My Fingers
CMIIW	<-- Correct Me If I'm Wrong
COI	<-- Come On In
CRAP	<-- Cheap Redundant Assorted Products
CRAWS	<-- Can't Remember Anything Worth A S**t
CTO	<-- Chief Talent Officer
CU2	<-- **See YoU Too**
CUA	<-- Commonly Used Acronyms
CUIC	<-- **See You** In Church
CUL8R	<-- **See You Later**
CWOX	<-- Complete Waste Of **Time**
CWYL	<-- Chat With You Later
CYA	<-- **See Ya/** Cover Your Ass
CYPUWIPD	<-- Can You Pick-Up What I'm Putting Down?

25

D

D/L	<-- DownLoad	**DL3B**	<-- Don't Let the Bad Bugs Byte
DARFC	<-- Ducking And Running For Cover	**DLTM**	<-- Don't Lie To Me
DBAI	<-- Designed By An Idiot	**DMM**	<-- Don't Make Me
DBEYR	<-- Don't Believe Everything You Read	**DND**	<-- Do Not Disturb
		DNS	<-- Domain Name Service
Dced	<-- Disconnected	**DNO**	<-- Don't KNOw
DD	<-- Dear Daughter	**DOS**	<-- Dead Operating System
DDN	<-- Defense Data Network	**DQMOT**	<-- Don't Quote Me On This
DDZ	<-- Dreaded Disease		
DEC	<-- Do Expect Cuts	**DQYDJ**	<-- Don't Quit Your Day Job
DEGT	<-- Don't Even Go There		
DETI	<-- Don't Even Think It	**DRIB**	<-- Don't Read If Busy
DHYB	<-- Don't Hold Your Breath	**DSH**	<-- Desperately Seeking Help
DGA	<-- Digital Guardian Angel	**DTC**	<-- Damn This Computer
DGARA	<-- Don't Give A Rats Ass	**DUCT**	<-- Did You See That?
DIIK	<-- Darn If I Know	**DWAI**	<-- Don't Worry About It
DILLIGAS	<-- Do I Look Like I Give A S**t	**DWAN**	<-- Don't Write A Novel
		DWISNWID	<-- Do What I Say Not What I Do
DIKU	<-- Do I Know You?		
DITY	<-- Did I Tell You	**DYJHIW**	<-- Don't You Just Hate It When…
DIY	<-- Do It Yourself		
DKDC	<-- Don't Know Don't Care	**DYTS**	<-- Don't You Think So?

E

E2E   <-- End-To-End

E3   <-- Electronic
       Entertainment Expo

EAK   <-- Eating At Keyboard

ECN   <-- Electronic
       Communication Network

ECP   <-- Excessive Cross Posting

EDGE   <-- Enhanced Data Rate
       For Global Evolution

EDI   <-- Electronic Data
       Interchange

EFF   <-- Electronic Frontier
       Foundation

EG   <-- Evil Grin

EIE   <-- Enough Is Enough

EMFJI   <-- Excuse Me For
       Jumping In

EMML   <-- E-Mail Me Later

EMP   <-- Excessive Multiple
       Posting

EMP   <-- Excessive Multiple
       Posting ;)

EMSG   <-- Email Message

EOD   <-- End Of Discussion

EOF   <-- End Of File

EOL   <-- End Of Lecture/
       End Of Line

EOM   <-- End Of Message

EOQ   <-- End Of Quote

EOT   <-- End Of Thread

EPIC   <-- Electronic Privacy
       Information Center

ENQ   <-- ENQuire

ESO   <-- Equipment Smarter
       than Operator

ETLA   <-- Extended Three
       Letter Acronym

EULA   <-- End-User
       License Agreement

EMWI   <-- E-Mailing While
       Intoxicated

EZ   <-- Easy :)

F

F	<-- Female	FOCL	<-- Falling Off Chair
F2F	<-- Face TO Face		Laughing
FAB	<-- Features Attributes	FOS	<-- Freedom Of Speech
	Benefits	FPS	<-- For Pete's Sake/
FAFWOA	<-- For A Friend		Frames Per Second
	WithOut Access	FRED	<-- F**king Ridiculous
FAQ	<-- Frequently Asked		Electronic Device
	Questions	FTP	<-- File Transfer Protocol
FAWC	<-- For Anyone Who Cares	FTTC	<-- Fiber To The Curb
FBKS	<-- Failure Between	FT2T	<-- From Time TO Time
	Keyboard & Seat	FU	<-- F**k yoU
FBOW	<-- For Better Or Worse	FUA	<-- Frequently Used
FBTW	<-- Fine Be That Way		Acronym/
FCOL	<-- For Crying Out Loud		F**k yoU Again
FCFS	<-- First Come First Served	FUBAR	<-- F**ked Up Beyond
FE	<-- Fatal Error		All Recognition
FFA	<-- Free For All	FUD	<-- Fear, Uncertainty
FIFO	<-- First In First Out		& Doubt
FIIK	<-- F**k If I Know	FURTB	<-- Full Up Ready
FIGJAM	<-- F**k I'm Good-		To Burst
	Just Ask Me	FWIW	<-- For What It's Worth
FISH	<-- First In Still Here	FYA	<-- For Your
FITB	<-- Fill In The Blank		Amusement
FOAF	<-- Friend Of A Friend	FYEO	<-- For Your Eyes Only
FOC	<-- Free Of Charge	FYI	<-- For Your Information

G

G1	<-- Good One	**GL!**	<-- Good Luck!
G2G	<-- Got To Go	**GL&GH**	<-- Good Luck
G4C	<-- Going For Coffee		and Good Hunting
GAFIA	<-- Get Away From It All	**GLYASDI**	<-- God Loves You
GAL	<-- Get A Life		And So Do I
GASP	<-- Go Away Silly Person	**GM**	<-- Good Morning
GB	<-- Giga Byte	**GMAB**	<-- Give Me A Break
GBH&K	<-- Great Big Hug	**GMAO**	<-- Giggling My Ass Off
	and Kisses	**GMBO**	<-- Giggling My Butt Off
GBR	<-- Garbled Beyond	**GMPY**	<-- GruMPY
	Recovery	**GNBL4Y**	<-- Got Nothing But
GD&R	<-- Grinning Ducking		Love For You
	And Running	**GR8MTA**	<-- Great Minds
GF	<-- Girl Friend		Think Alike
GFAK	<-- Go Fly A Kite	**GO**	<-- Get Out
GFR	<-- Grim File Reaper	**GOB**	<-- Good 'Ol Boy
GG	<-- Good Game/Gotta Go	**GOI**	<-- Get Over It
GGN	<-- Gotta Go Now	**GOOH**	<-- Get Out Of Here
GGU2	<-- Good Game yoU Two	**GOOMF**	<-- Get Out Of My Face
GIGO	<-- Garbage In	**GOK**	<-- God Only Knows
	Garbage Out	**GRRR**	<-- Growling ;)
GIRO	<-- Garbage In	**GTSY**	<-- Glad To See You
	Rubbish Out		
GIWIST	<-- Gee-I Wish I'd		
	Said That		
GJ!	<-- Good Job!		

H

H/O	<-- Hold On	HMS	<-- Hanging My Self
HABU	<-- Have A Better `Un	HMT	<-- Here's My Try
HAGN	<-- Have A Good Night	HMWK	<-- HoMeWorK
HAG1	<-- Have A Good One	HOAS	<-- Hold On A Second
HAHA	<-- Having A Heart Attack	HOHA	<-- Hollywood Hacker
		HORU	<-- How Old Are You?
HAND	<-- Have A Nice Day	HSIK	<-- How Should I Know?
HAK	<-- Hug And Kiss	HTH	<-- Hope This Helps
HD	<-- HolD	HTSI	<-- Hope That Sinks In
HH	<-- Holding Hands	HUA	<-- Heads Up Ace
HRB	<-- HuRry Back	HUYA	<-- Head Up Your Ass
HVF	<-- HaVe Fun	HWMBI	<-- He Who Must Be Ignored
HHIS	<-- Hanging Head In Shame		
HHOK	<-- Ha Ha-Only Kidding		
HIG	<-- How's It Going?		
HIH	<-- Hope It Helps		
HILIACACLO	<-- Help I Lapsed Into A Coma And Can't Log Off!		
HIOOC	<-- Help! I'm Out Of Coffee		
HIWTH	<-- Hate It When That Happens		
HLM	<-- He Loves Me		
HMPZ	<-- Help Me Please		

I

IAE	<-- In Any Event	IME	<-- In My Experience
IAG	<-- It's All Good	IMPOV	<-- In My Point Of View
IAGW	<-- In A Good Way	IMP	<-- I Might Be Pregnant
IANAL	<-- I Am Not A Lawyer	IMO	<-- In My Opinion
IBM	<-- Idiots Bought Me	INPO	<-- In No Particular Order
IBT	<-- In Between Technology	IOW	<-- In Other Words
IBTC	<-- Itty Bitty Titty Commitee	IRL	<-- In Real Life
IC	<-- I See	IRSTBO	<-- It Really Sucks The Big One
ICMP	<-- Internet Control Message Protocol	ISP	<-- Internet Service Provider
ICOC	<-- I Could Of Course	ISRY	<-- I'm SoRrY
IDBI	<-- I Don't Believe It	ISS	<-- It's So Simple
IDC	<-- I Don't Care	ISTM	<-- It Seems To Me
IDGI	<-- I Don't Get It	ITIA	<-- It's The Information Age
IDK	<-- I Don't Know		
IDM	<-- It Doesn't Matter	ITRO	<-- In The Reality Of
IFU	<-- I F**ked Up	ITSFWI	<-- If The Shoe FitsWear It
IHU	<-- I Hate YoU		
II	<-- I'm Impressed	IVL	<-- In Virtual Life
IIRC	<-- If I Recall Correctly	IWALU	<-- I Will Always Love YoU
IKWUM	<-- I Know What You Mean		
		IWBIWISI	<-- I Will Believe It When I See It
ILIC	<-- I Laughed I Cried		
ILY	<-- I Love You	IYD	<-- In Your Dreams
IM	<-- Immediate Message/ Instant Message	IYKWIM	<-- If You Know What I Mean

J

J/C	<-- Just Checking	JT	<-- Just Teasing
J/W	<-- Just Wondering	JTLYK	<-- Just To Let You Know
J4G	<-- Just FOR Grins		
J4SAG	<-- Just For S**ts And Grins	JW	<-- Just Wondering
J6P	<-- Joe SIX-Pack		
JAFO	<-- Just Another F**king Onlooker		
JAM	<-- Just A Minute		
JAS	<-- Just A Second		
JASE	<-- Just Another System Error		
JAWS	<-- Just Another Windows Shell		
JBOD	<-- Just A Bunch Of Disks		
JIC	<-- Just In Case		
JIT	<-- Just In Time		
JJWY	<-- Just Joking With You		
JK	<-- Just Kidding		
JM2C	<-- Just My TWO Cents		
JMO	<-- Just My Opinion		
JMHO	<-- Just My Humble Opinion		
JOOTT	<-- Just One Of Those Things		
JP	<-- Just Playing		

K

K	<-- Ok	**KYPO**	<-- Keep Your Pants On
KB	<-- Kiss Back		
KBD	<-- KeyBoarD		
KEWL	<-- Cool ;)		
KFY	<-- Kiss For You		
KHYF	<-- Know How You Feel		
KIF	<-- Knowledge Interchange Format		
KIQ	<-- Keep It Quiet		
KISS	<-- Keep It Simple Stupid		
KIT	<-- Keep In Touch		
KITB	<-- Kick In The Butt		
KMA	<-- Kiss My Ass		
KMG	<-- Kiss My Grits		
KMYF	<-- Kiss Me You Fool		
KOC	<-- Kiss On Cheek		
KOK	<-- KnOcK		
KOL	<-- Kiss On Lips		
KOTC	<-- Kiss On The Cheek		
KOTL	<-- Kiss On The Lips		
KUTGS	<-- Keep Up The Good Spirit		
KUTGW	<-- Keep Up The Good Work		
KWIM	<-- Know What I Mean?		

L

2L&P	<-- Live Long & Prosper	L2OL	<-- Laughing Out Outrageously Loud
L8R G8R	<-- Later Gator		
LAB	<-- Life's A Bummer	LOML	<-- Light Of My Life
LABTYD	<-- Life's A Bitch Then You Die	LOPSOD	<-- Long On Promises Short On Delivery
LAN	<-- Local Area Network	LTIC	<-- Laughing Till I Cry
LAQ	<-- Lame Ass Quote	LTNS	<-- Long Time No See
LART	<-- Loser Attitude Readjustment Tool	LTNT	<-- Long Time No Type
		LTR	<-- Long Term Relationship
LAY	<-- Looking At You		
LD	<-- Long Distance	LUB	<-- Laughing Under Breath
LHO	<-- Laughing Head Off		
LIFO	<-- Last In First Out	LULAS	<-- Love YoU Like A Sister
LIS	<-- Lost In Space		
LISP	<-- Lots Of Infuriating Silly People	LWR	<-- Launch When Ready
		LYK	<-- Let You Know
LLAL	<-- Laughing Like A Lunatic	LYLY	<-- Love You & Leave You
LMA	<-- Leave Me Alone		
LMBO	<-- Laughing My Butt Off		
LMC	<-- Let Me See		
LMK	<-- Let Me Know		
LOA	<-- Love On Arrival		
LOIS	<-- Laughing On the InSide		
LOL	<-- Laughing Out Loud		

M

M	<-- Male	MOO	<-- Mud Object-Oriented
M2F	<-- More TO Follow	MOSS	<-- Member Of The Same Sex
M8	<-- Mate		
MAC	<-- Most Applications Crash	MOTD	<-- Message Of The Day
		MOTOS	<-- Member Of The Opposite Sex
MAN	<-- Metropolitan Area Network		
		MPTY	<-- More Power To You
MAPI	<-- Messaging Application Programming Interface	MR	<-- Modem Ready
		MSG	<-- Message
MB	<-- Mega Byte	MTFBWY	<-- May The Force Be With You
MEG	<-- Mega Evil Grin		
MFD	<-- Multi Function Device	MUAK	<-- Smooch ;)
MHB4Y	<-- My Heart Bleeds For You	MUG	<-- Multi User Game
		MUSH	<-- Multi User Shared Hallucination
MHOTY	<-- My Hat's Off To You		
MIASGB	<-- Make It A Short GoodBye	MUSM	<-- Miss yoU So Much
		MYOB	<-- Mind Your Own Business
MIL	<-- Mother In Law		
MIME	<-- Multipurpose Internet Mail Extensions		
MIPS	<-- Meaningless Indication Of Processor Speed		
MLA	<-- Multiple LetterAcronym		
MP	<-- Moral Police		

N

N	<-- IN	NGI	<-- Next-Generation
N/A	<-- Not Applicable/		Internet
	Not Affiliated	NHTOB	<-- Never Heard That
N/T	<-- No Text		One Before
N1	<-- Nice One	NIC	<-- Networked Information
N2M	<-- Not TO Much		Center
N2S	<-- Needless TO Say	NIM	<-- No Internal Message
NADT	<-- Not A Darn Thing	NIMBY	<-- Not In My Back Yard
NAFAIK	<-- Not As Far As	NIME	<-- Not In My Experience
	I Know	NITS	<-- Nervous In The
NAK	<-- Nursing At Keyboard		Service
NALOP	<-- Not A Lot Of People	NOM	<-- No Offense Meant
NAP	<-- Network Access Point	NONYAB	<-- None YA Business
NAZ	<-- Name Address Zip	NOP	<-- NO Problem
NB	<-- Nota Bene	NPNG	<-- No Pain No Gain
NBD	<-- No Big Deal	NREN	<-- National Research and
NBIF	<-- No Basis In Fact		Education Network
NC	<-- No Comment	NRG	<-- ENeRGy
NCG	<-- New College Graduate	NSS	<-- No S**t Sherlock
NE1	<-- Anyone	NTYMI	<-- Now That You
NEM	<-- Nothing Else Matters		Mention It
NETUA	<-- Nobody Ever Tells	NVRM	<-- NeVeR Mind
	Us Anything	NVNG	<-- Nothing Ventured-
NFI	<-- No F**king Idea		Nothing Gained
NG	<-- New Game		

O

OAO	<-- Over And Out	**OOSOOM**	<-- Out Of Sight
OAUS	<-- On An Unrelated		Out Of Mind
	Subject	**OOT**	<-- Out Of Town
OB	<-- Obligatory	**OOTB**	<-- Out Of The Box /
OBTW	<-- Oh –By The Way		Out Of The Blue
OEM	<-- Original Equipment	**OPS!**	<-- Oh People Stop!
	Manufacturer	**ORN**	<-- Oh Really Now
OFIS	<-- On Floor With Stitches	**OS**	<-- Operating System
OH	<-- Off Hook	**OS/2**	<-- Obsolete Soon Too
OIC	<-- Oh I See	**OSOM**	<-- Out of Sight Out
OJ	<-- Only Joking/		of Mind
	Orange Juice ;)	**OT**	<-- Off Topic/Other Topic
	Guilty :-a	**OTOH**	<-- On The Other Hand
OK	<-- **All Correct ;)**	**OTT**	<-- Over The Top
OL	<-- Old Lady **<--** Wife	**OTTOMH**	<-- Off The Top
OLGA	<-- OnLine Guitar Archive		Of My Head
OM	<-- Old Man <-- Husband	**OTW**	<-- On The Way
OMDB	<-- Over My Dead Body	**OUSU**	<-- Oh You Shut Up
OMG	<-- Oh My God	**OWTTE**	<-- Or Words To
OMIK	<-- Open Mouth Insert		That Effect
	Keyboard	**OY VEY**	<-- **Oh No! Kapeesh?**
OMKC	<-- On My Knees Crying		
ONNA	<-- Oh No Not Again		
OOC	<-- Out Of Character		
OOI	<-- Out Of Interest		
OOP	<-- Out Of Production		

P

PABG	<-- Pack A Big Gun	**PLZ**	<-- Please
PANS	<-- Pretty Awesome New Stuff	**PM**	<-- Private Message
		PMJI	<-- Pardon My Jumping In
PAW	<-- Parents Are Watching	**PMS**	<-- Pretty Much Sucks
PCMCIA	<-- People Can't Memorize Computer Industry Acronyms	**POAHF**	<-- Put On A Happy Face
		POETS	<-- Piss On Everything Tomorrow's Saturday
PD	<-- Public Domain	**PONA**	<-- Person Of No Account
PDA	<-- Public Display of Affection	**POP**	<-- Point Of Presence
		POS	<-- Parent Over Shoulder
PDE	<-- Puppy Dog Eyed	**POTB**	<-- Pats On The Back
PDOMA	<-- Pulled Directly Out of My Ass	**POTC**	<-- Peck On The Cheek
		POTS	<-- Plain Old Telephone Service
PDQ	<-- Pretty Damned Quick		
PDS!	<-- Please Don't Shoot!	**POV**	<-- Point Of View
PEBCAK	<-- Problem Exists Between Chair And Keyboard	**PPL**	<-- PeoPLe
		PPP	<-- Petty Pet Peeve
		PS	<-- Post Script/Pit Stop
PEST	<-- Please Excuse Slow Typing	**PSA**	<-- Public Show of Affection
PIAK	<-- Slap In The Face	**PU**	<-- That Stinks! ;)
PIMP	<-- Peeing In My Pants		
PITA	<-- Pain In The Ass		
PLUR	<-- Peace Love Unity Respect		
PLOKTA	<-- Press Lots Of Keys To Abort		

Q

Q&A	<-- **Q**uestions **& A**nswers
Q4U	<-- **Q**uestion **F**or Yo**U**
QDSM	<-- **Q**uick & **D**irty
	Solution **M**anager
QL	<-- **Q**uit **L**aughing
QOS	<-- **Q**uality **O**f **S**ervice
QS	<-- **Q**uit **S**crolling
QSL	<-- **R**eply
QSO	<-- **C**onversation
QT	<-- **Cutie**
QWERTY	<-- **Keyboard**
QWTL	<-- **Q**uit **L**aughing

R

R   <-- **Are**

R4D   <-- Request **For D**iscussion

R4I   <-- Request **For** Info

R&D   <-- Research **&**
           Development

R&R   <-- Rest **&** Relaxation

RAEBNC <-- Read And Enjoyed
           But No Comment

RAM   <-- Random-Access
           Memory

RAW   <-- Rules As Written

RBAY   <-- Right Back At Ya

RBTL   <-- Read Between
           The Lines

Rced   <-- ReConnected

RE   <-- Regards

RI&W   <-- Read It & Weep

RIP   <-- Rest In Peace

RITY   <-- AlRIghTY

RL   <-- Real Life

RLF   <-- Real Life Friends

RME   <-- Rolling My Eyes

RML   <-- Read My Lips

RN!   <-- Right Now!

ROFL   <-- Rolling On Floor
           Laughing

ROTFLMAO   <-- Rolling On The
           Floor Laughing
           My Ass Off

ROS   <-- Run-Of-Site

ROTM   <-- Right On The Money

RPG   <-- Role Playing Games

RSN   <-- Real Soon Now

RVD   <-- Really Very Dumb

RU   <-- Are YoU?

RUOK   <-- Are YoU OK?

RTFAQ   <-- Read The FAQ

RTK   <-- Return To Keyboard

RTSM   <-- Read The Stupid
           Manual

RWT   <-- Repeat Whole Thing

RYO   <-- Roll Your Own
           --> Write Your Own
           Program

RZN   <-- **Reason**

S

S	<-- Sigh or Smile	SIIC	<-- See If I Care
S^	<-- What'S Up	SIL	<-- Sister In Law
S2R	<-- Send TO Receive	SIMCA	<-- Sitting In My
S&N	<-- Smile And Nod		Chair Amused
SAMAGAL	<-- Stop Annoying Me	SITD	<-- Still In The Dark
	And Get A Life	SLIRK	<-- Smart Little Rich Kid
SASB	<-- Sobbing And	SMAO	<-- Showing My Ass Off
	Sniffing Bitterly	SMOFF	<-- Serious Mode OFF
SCNR	<-- Sorry Could Not Resist	SMOP	<-- Small Matter Of
SCSI	<-- System Can't See It		Programming
SED	<-- Said Enough Darling	SNAFU	<-- Situation Normal All
SETE	<-- Smiling Ear To Ear		F**ked Up
SF	<-- Surfer Friendly	SNAG	<-- Sensitive New Age Guy
SFAIAA	<-- So Far As I Am Aware	SNERT	<-- Snotty Nosed
SFLA	<-- Stupid Four		Egotistical Rotten
	Letter Acronym		Teenager
SFSG	<-- So Far So Good	SOMY	<-- Sick Of Me Yet?
SHIC	<-- So Happy I Could…	SOP	<-- Stay Off the Pipe
SHID	<-- Slaps Head In Disgust	SPAM	<-- Stupid Persons'
SHMILY	<-- See How Much		AdvertiseMent
	I Love You	SRY	<-- SoRrY
SHTSI	<-- Somebody Had	SSDD	<-- Same S**t
	To Say It		Different Day
SHUP	<-- Shut Up	SSEWBA	<-- Someday Soon
SIC	<-- Sitting In Chair		Everything Will Be
SIG	<-- Special Interest Group		Acronyms ;)

T

TA   <-- Thanks Again

TAFN   <-- That's All For Now

TAFT   <-- That's A Frightening Thought

TAH   <-- Take A Hike

TANJ   <-- There Ain't No Justice

TARFU   <-- Things Are Really F**ked Up

TAT   <-- Turn Around Time

TBNT   <-- Thanx But No Thanx

TCB   <-- Trouble Came Back

TCOY   <-- Take Care Of Yourself

TEOTWAWKI   <-- The End Of The World As We Know It

TFDS   <-- That's For Damn Sure

TFH   <-- Thread From Hell

TGAL   <-- Think Globally Act Locally

TGIF   <-- Thank God Its Friday

TIC   <-- Tongue In Cheek

TIIC   <-- The Idiots In Charge

TILII   <-- Tell It Like It Is

TLA   <-- Three Letter Acronym

TLGO   <-- The List Goes On

TLK2UL8R   <-- TaLK TO YoU Later

TMA   <-- Take My Advice

TMI   <-- To Much Information

TNSTAAFL   <-- There's No Such Thing As A Free Lunch

TNT   <-- Till Next Time

TNX   <-- ThaNks

TOBAL   <-- There Oughta Be A Law...

TOBG   <-- This Oughta Be Good

TOPCA   <-- Til Our Paths Cross Again

TOY   <-- Thinking Of You

TSOH   <-- Total Sense Of Humour

TWHAB   <-- This Won't Hurt A Bit

TWIWI   <-- That Was Interesting Wasn't It

TWMA   <-- Till We Meet Again

TYCLO   <-- Turn Your Caps Lock Off

U

U	<-- yoU
U/L	<-- UpLoad
U2	<-- YoU TOO
UAE	<-- Unrecoverable Application Error
UAPITA	<-- YoU're A Pain In The Ass
UBD	<-- User Brain Damage
UCCOM	<-- YoU Can Count On Me
UCE	<-- Unsolicited Commercial E-Mail
UIAM	<-- Unless I Am Mistaken
UOM$	<-- YoU Owe Me Money
UR	<-- YoU aRe
URL	<--Uniform Resource Locator
UR2Y4M	<-- YoU Are Too Wise For Me
URAQT!	<-- YoU Are A Cutie!
UTSL	<-- Use The Source Luke
URWLCM	<-- YoU're WeLCoMe
URYY4M	<-- YoU aRe Too Wise For Me

V

VBG	<-- Very Big Grin
VEG	<-- Very Evil Grin
VES	<-- Very Evil Smile
VF$	<-- Value For Money
VM	<-- Voice Mail
VNP	<-- Vulcan Nerve Pinch
VPN	<-- Virtual Private Network
VR	<-- Virtual Reality
VWD	<-- Very Well Done
VWG	<-- Very Wicked Grin
VWS	<-- Very Wicked Smile

W

W^	<-- What's UP	WN1GNB4	<-- Were No One Has
W2MI	<-- Way TO Much Info		GoNe Before
W3	<-- World Wide Web	WOB	<-- Waste Of Bandwidth
W8	<-- Wait	WOE	<-- World Of
WAB	<-- What A Bummer		Entertainment
WAD	<-- Without A Doubt	WOG	<-- Wise Old Guy
WAG	<-- Wild Ass Guess	WOMBAT	<-- Waste Of Money
WAI	<-- What An Idiot		Brains And Time
WAM	<-- Wait A Minute	WR2	<-- With Respect TO
WASP	<-- Wireless Application	WRUF	<-- Where aRe yoU From?
	Service Providers	WSLS	<-- Win Some Lose Some
WAYD	<-- What Are You Doing?	WTGP	<-- Want To Go Private
WB	<-- Welcome Back	WTTC	<-- Welcome To The Club
WBS	<-- Write Back Soon	WTY	<-- Waving To You
WDALYIC	<-- Who Died And Left	WU2M	<-- Will YoU Marry Me?
	You In Charge	WWYL	<-- When Will You Learn?
WDOI	<-- Wouldn't Dream Of It	WX4ME	<-- Works FOR ME
WDYM	<-- What Do You Mean?	WYMOWS	<-- Wash Your Mouth
WGACA	<-- What Goes Around		Out With Soap
	Comes Around	WYP	<-- What's Your Problem?
WGAS	<-- Who Gives A S**t	WYSIWYG	<-- What You See Is
WIBNI	<-- Wouldn't It Be Nice If		What You Get
WIIFM	<-- What's In It For Me		
WISP	<-- Winning Is So		
	Pleasurable		
WIT	<-- Wordsmith In Training		

X

X	<-- Times/EX
XO	<-- Hugs & Kisses
XQZME	<-- Excuse Me
XTLA	<-- EXtended Three Letter Acronym
XYL	<-- EX Young Lady

Y

/YD	<-- YesterDay
2YZ4U	<-- Two Wise For YoU
3Y	<-- Yeah Yeah Yeah
Y	<-- WhY?
Y2K	<-- You're Too Kind/ Year 2000
Y3T	<-- You Telling The Truth
YABA	<-- Yet Another Bloody Acronym
YAFIYGI	<-- You Asked For It You Got It
YATB	<-- You Are The Best
YBKNG^	<-- You're BreaKiNG Up
YGBK	<-- You Gotta Be Kiddin'
YGLT	<-- You're Gonna Love This
YKYARW	<-- You Know You're A Redneck When...
YKYBOTLW	<-- You Know You've Been Online Too Long When...
YMMV	<-- Your Mileage May Vary
YNG	<-- YouNG
YWIA	<-- You're Welcome In Advance
YWN2XOME	<-- You Want To Kiss & Hug ME
YOYO	<-- You're On Your Own

Z

Z$S	<-- Zero **Money** Spent
ZA	<-- Zero Administration
ZAV	<-- Zero Added Value
ZZZ	<-- **Sleeping**

misc

@	<-- **AT**
$	<-- **Money**
?	<-- **Huh?**
?4U	<-- **Question For** YoU
^5	<-- **High Five**
>U	<-- **Screw** YoU!
123ABC	<-- **Talk About School**
2B	<-- **To Be**
2L8	<-- **To Late**
2U2	<-- **To** YoU **Too**
404	<-- **I Haven't A Clue**
4EVR	<-- **ForEVR**
4UNO	<-- **For** All YoU KNOw
4U	<-- **For** YoU
20	<-- **Location**
100	<-- **Nature Calls/Pit Stop**
=w=	<-- **Whatever**
poof	<-- **Left The Chat Room**

Return Codes

A Server Message you might see when surfing <-- reports the **Return** status of a Web page.

Success   ## *Failed*

200 <-- OK   400 <-- Bad Request

201 <-- Created   401 <-- Unauthorized

202 <-- Accepted   402 <-- Payment Required

203 <-- Partial Information   403 <-- Forbidden

204 <-- No Response   404 <-- Not Found

300 <-- Redirected   500 <-- Internal Error

301 <-- Moved   501 <-- Not Implemented

302 <-- Found   502 <-- Overloaded Temporarily

303 <-- New Method   503 <-- Gateway Timeout

304 <-- Not Modified

Decoding Complete!
B^)

<-- | White Space <-- use it...
   V

Siliconia

})i({

= **Geographical Nicknames**:

Relates to Cities/Areas that are swimming in high-tech businesses so

Tour On:

Automation Alley	<-- **Oakland County, Michigan,**
Billy-Can Valley	<-- **Arnhem Land**, northern **Australia**
Biotech Beach	<-- **Orange County, California,**
Bit Valley	<-- Vague area in **Japan**
CWM Silicon	<-- **Newport, Gwent, South Wales**
Cyberabad	<-- City of **Hyderabad, Andhra Pradesh, India**
Cyberchella Valley	<-- **Coachella Valley** from **Palm Springs** to **Thermal, California**
Cyberdistrict	<-- **Boston, Massachusetts**
Digital Coast	<-- Coast south from **Ventura, California**
Digital Rhine	<-- The **Over-the-Rhine** areaof **Cincinnati, Ohio**
Dot Bowl	<-- **Silicon Valley, California**
Dot Commonwealth	<-- **Massachusetts**
DSP Valley	<-- Area around the **University** of **Leuven, Belgium**
E-Coast	<-- **Portsmouth, New Hampshire**
E-Country	<-- **Fairfax County, Virginia**
Flanders Language Valley	<-- Area between **Antwerp** and **Brussels, Belgium**
Hollywired	<-- **Hollywood, California**

India's Silicon Valley **<-- Bangalore, India**

Intelligent Island <-- **Singapore**

Kiselsta <-- **Kista**, a suburb of **Stockholm, Sweden**

Media Del Rey <-- **Santa Monica / Marina Del Rey, California**

Multimedia Gulch <-- The area **south of Market Street**
San Francisco, California

Multimedia Super Corridor <-- Area south of **Kuala Lumpur**,
Malaysia

Philicon Valley <-- Western suburbs centered around
Valley Forge and **Wayne**
Philadelphia, Pennsylvania

Silicon Alley <-- **Broadway** from the
Flatiron District to TriBeCa
New York City, New York

Silicon Alps <-- **Carinthia, Austria**

Silicon Bayou <-- **Boca Raton, Florida/Louisiana**

Silicon Beach <-- **Florida/Santa Barbara, California**

Silicon Bog <-- The midlands of **Ireland**

Silicon City <-- **Chicago, Illinois**

Silicon Desert <-- **Phoenix, Arizona**

Silicon Ditch <-- The **M4 Corridor**, west out of **London**

Silicon Dominion <-- State of **Virginia**

Silicon Fen <-- **Cambridge, England**

Silicon Freeway <-- Southern **California**

Silicon Forest <-- To the west Area around Route 26
Portland, Oregon
Seattle, Washington <--The overall
Puget Sound area

Touring... 8^)

Silicon Forest Australia	**<-- Eastern Australia**
Silicon Glacier	<-- The region around **Kalispell, Montana**
Silicon Glen	<-- The region around **Livingston, Scotland** also applied more generally to the entire stretch from **Edinburgh to Glasgow**
Silicon Gulch	<-- **Austin, Texas** **San Jose, California**
Silicon Hill	<-- Area around **Hudson, Massachusetts**
Silicon Hills	<-- **Austin, Texas** <-- The hills west of downtown
Silicon Hollow	<-- **Oak Ridge, Tennessee**
Silicon Holler	<-- **Northern Virginia** suburbs of **Washington D.C.,**
Silicon Island	<-- **Whidbey Island, Washington** **Taiwan,** Republic of China **Alameda, California** **Long Island, New York** **St. John, Virgin Islands**
Silicon Isle	<-- **Ireland**
Silicon Mesa	<-- **North Albuquerque** **Rio Rancho** area of **New Mexico**
Silicon Mountain	<-- **Hudson, Massachusetts** **Colorado Springs, Colorado** **Mountaintop, Pennsylvania**
Silicon Necklace	<-- **Boston, Massachusetts** suburbs
Silicon Orchard	<-- **Wenatchee Valley, Washington**
Silicon Parkway	<-- Area around the **Merritt** and **Wilbur Cross** Parkways, **Connecticut** **Garden State Parkway, New Jersey**
Silicon Plain	<-- **Kempele, Finland**

Silicon Plains	<-- **Atadim Park**, in north **Tel Aviv, Israel**
	Lincoln, Nebraska
Silicon Plantation	<-- State of **Virginia**
Silicon Plateau	<-- **Bangalore, India**
Silicon Polder	<-- **The Netherlands**
Silic_n Prairie	<-- **Ed Bluestein Boulevard, Austin, Texas**
	Iowa City / Fairfield vicinity, **Iowa**
	Sioux Falls vicinity, **South Dakota**
	Urbana/Champaign area of **Illinois**
	Richardson, Texas
	Chicago, Illinois North and/
	or Northwest suburbs
	Area around **Minneapolis /**
	St. Paul, Minnesota
	Payne County, Oklahoma
	Kansas City, Missouri
	Lincoln, Nebraska
Silicon Rain Forest	<-- **Seattle, Washington**
Silicon River	<--Broad band through the **Kansas City –**
	Columbia - St. Louis Corridor
	in **Missouri**
Silicon Sandbar	<-- **Cape Cod, Massachusetts**
Silicon Saxony	<-- The eastern state of **Saxony, Germany**
Silicon Seaboard	<-- **Richmond, Virginia**
Silicon Snow bank	<-- Area around **Minneapolis /**
	St. Paul, Minnesota,
Silicon Spires	<-- **Oxford, England**
Silicon Swamp	<-- **Perry, Florida**
	Indiantown, Florida

Still Touring... 8^)

Silicon Triangle	<-- Area around **Raleigh / Durham, North Carolina**
Silicon Tundra	<-- Area around **Minneapolis / St. Paul, Minnesota**
	Area around **Ottawa, Canada**
Silicon Valais	<-- **Valais, Switzerland**
Silicon Valley	<-- **San Jose, California** and surroundings
Silicon Valley North	<-- Area around **Ottawa, Canada**
Silicon Valley of the East	<-- **Penang State, Malaysia**
Silicon Valley Forge	<-- **Philadelphia, Pennsylvania**
Silicon Village	<-- **Scotts Valley, California**
	North Adams, Massachusetts
Silicon Vineyard	<-- **Petaluma / Santa Rosa / Napa Valley, California**
	Okanagan Valley, British Columbia
Silicon Wadi	<-- **Israel**
Silicorn Valley	<-- **Fairfield, Iowa**
Siliwood	<-- **Hollywood, California**
Teknopolis	<-- Greater **Johor Bahru** city, **Johor State, Malaysia**
Telecom Beach	<-- **San Diego, California**
Telecom Corridor	<-- **Richardson, Texas**
Telecom Valley	<-- **The Riviera, France**
	Catawba County, North Carolina
	Minas Gerais, Brazil
Webport	<-- **Portland, Maine**

Cyber Tour Complete!
8^"

Word List
B^)

Need I explain?

Ok, only if U insist --> this glossary is compiled of specialized Netizen terms that I thought would be cool for U 2 know. I have parsed the definitions so processing <-- I hope --> will be smooth.

Above The Fold: The Web page that is visible without scrolling.

Acronyms: I thought we went over this --> Remember Shortys?

Agent: A program that does things for you <-- like locating favorite sites or checking e-mail.

Alpha Geek = Coolest Geek

Alpha Pup = Coolest Netizen

Alt or Alt. : Alt-Dot <-- these are newsgroups that discuss **Alternative** subjects.

Apollo Syndrome: Example --> C'mon it's time to clean the house --> Just a minute let me finish this level --> and this game goes on and on and on...

Analog: The opposite of digital.

Angry Garden Salad: Poorly designed Web site GUI with incorrect code behind it.

Animersive: A bad designed entertainment portal mess with all sorts of cool serviceability.

Anomaly: A computer bug.

Anticipointment: The bummed out feeling when something does not live up to its own hype.

Any Key: Newbies --> PAY ATTENTION <-- **Any Key** is Not on the keyboard <-- it means exactly what it means ;)

ASCII: **A**merican **S**tandard **C**ode for **I**nformation **I**nterchange <-- basically --> the code numbers used by computers to represent all the uppercase and lowercase Latin letters, numbers, punctuation, and other symbols. Look for Galleries of ASCII Art on the net.

ASCII Art: An **Art** form that uses **ASCII** characters.

ASCII Bashing: To rearrange the layout of the page in a text file.

ASCII-Armored: An encrypted message in ASCII so that it can be e-mailed normally.

Astroturf: A grassroots effort on the Net involving massive amounts of e-mail sent to politicians.

Audiocast: Live **Audio**/Video Broad**Cast**.

Avatar: A 3D actor <--or icon --> that represents who and where you are in the virtual world.

Backbone: Core of the Net.

Backdoor: Secret way into a Web site.

Back-Hack: Finding out who is hacking into a system.

Bailey The Switcher: Someone who attacks by altering the contents of other peoples' messages.

Bandwidth Hog: Anything that takes forever to download.

Bang = !

Bang The GUI: Consummating a program to know it inside and out.
Banner Blindness: A symptom of too many Ad Banners <-- so people tend to ignore them.

Barneyware: Anything <-- and I mean Anything with little or no substance.

BASIC: **B**ill's **A**ttempt to **S**eize **I**ndustry **C**ontrol

Baud Barf: The strange noises you hear when connecting to the net.

Bellhead: A Telecommunication professional.

Below The Fold: The content in the middle or bottom of a Web page that requires scrolling.

Beta Baby: A child born to a Techie after 1995.

Big Room: The real world <-- the room you return to after surfing the Net.

Bipolar Belief System: Two popular <-- opposite attitudes --> either the Net changes everything --><-- or the Net changes nothing.

Bit Bucket: Some place in cyberspace where missing file or documents <-- like e-mail --> end up.

BitLoss = Information Loss

BitStream = Information Flow

BlameStorming: It's all your fault.

Blatherer: Someone who types on and on and on and on <-- See the last rule of Netiquette.

Blogosphere: Where to Blog <-- keep an up-to-date e-journal of your thoughts to share with others.

Bloodware: Shareware that asks that you donate blood to Red Cross.

Blue Screen Of Death: =8-O <-- what to do if you see this on your computer! Then call CERT.

Boat anchor = Junk Hardware.

Body = Content

Bogus = Dumb = Stupid = Wrong

Bot = Software Ro**Bot** <-- Does tedious tasks that you request on the Computer or the Net.

Bounce: When your e-mail is returned instead of placed in the Bit Bucket.

Box = Computer

Bozo Filter: A program that filters e-mail messages and newsgroup postings from a Bozo.

Bozon: The smallest unit of stupidity.

Brain Drain: Suffered when Geeks, Techies or Nerds leave.

Brain Dump: Uploading all the information from your MeatJail.

Brain Fart: Uhhhhhhhhh... ... ... I forgot ... ... ?

Brandalism: The practice of defacing public spaces <-- like schools --> with advertisements.

Broadcast Storm: The Storm before a Network meltdown.

Brochureware: Site that looks like the company's **Brochure**.

Broken Pipe: When the download/data stream/**Pipe** has been **Broken**.

Bug: Your computer goes nuts from **A Software Error** byting its hardware.

Cached Out = Extremely Tired

Cancelbot: It looks for and deletes any postings from people or subjects that a master doesn't like.

Cancelbunny = Cancelpoodle: People who delete postings to newsgroups by claiming copyright violations.

Cancelmoose: Someone that wages a war against spamming.

Canon: Unlike Turklebuam this information is for real and official.

Careware: Shareware that requests a donation to a charity for payment.

Carnivore: FBI's e-mail surveillance tool <-- which is currently illegal?

Carpet Bomb: A message sent to every subscriber of a particular network <-- whether they want it or not.

Cascade: The series of replies received after posting a message.

Cell Mates: By using one touch dialing --> I thee wed.

Cell Phone: I think we should call it a Digi :)

Chat: Sending Text IMs to someone in Timbuktu & vice versa.

Chat Acronym: Haven't we been through this?

Chat Room Bob = Net Pervert <-- They seek and then send flirty messages to pretty faces but would never approach a Real Woman.

Chatfly = Cyber Barfly <-- they hang out in chat rooms <-- day in/day out and chat with anyone.

Chiphead: An old-time Computer Science Engineer.

Cipher = CipherText = Encrypted Text

Click-&-Mortar = Bricks-&-Clicks <-- Cyberspace and Carbon Community stores.

Clickly: Click quick.

Cluster Funk = X infinity things go wrong on a computer @ = X because of 1 action <-- or a room full of PU Programmers ;)

Cobweb Site: A dead Web page with broken links.

Computer Wiz: One who is brilliant at all things Computer.

Cookies: A text file with information about your computer that stores history like login/passwords and tracks your movements.

Core Competencies: Your best qualities. What RU good @?

Cornea Gumbo: A visually over cooked Web site.

Cracker: Someone <-- Not a Hacker! --> who **Cracks** security on a system or a software program <-- usually Shareware.

Crawler: Searches the Net for any new resources and then contributes the information to a database so that you can locate them with a search engine.

Crippleware = **Cripple** + Demo**ware** = $ to make software work.

Cross Post: To post a message to several newsgroups simultaneously.

Cryppie: A **Cryp**tographic software Hacker.

Crypto Rage = **Net Road Rage**

Cyberangels: Assists victims of Internet crimes.

Cybercad = **Cyber Lounge Lizard**

Cybercide: The killing of a person's Virtual Identity.

Cyberfraud = **Internet Fraud**

Cyberpunk: An anarchic young Programmer.

Cybernoir: Weird **Cyber Films** usually of B-grade quality.

Cybersex = **Text Sex** = Safe Sex for singles.

Cyberslacker: Those people that think Work X = Play X.

Cyberslang = **Geek Speak**

Cyberspace: You know W3 --> the Internet, Digital, and Cyber world.

Cyberterrorism: Any criminal attempt to disrupt computer or communications services.

Cybertourists: People who only surf on the weekends or holidays <-- this results in Wire Jams.

Cyberwar: Hacker attack on government computer systems <-- whereas --> the Hacker always chooses the battlefield and the Defender is usually unaware that they're being attacked.

Cybrarian 0= librarian <-- they make a living @ data searching and surfing.

Cytizen: A person who belongs to the Cyber world.

Cytizenship = Internet Citizen

Dag-Tag: End of message <-- then Screen Name <-- then + + + + + Bla Bla Bla <-- **+ Bla = Dag-Tag**

Data Dump = Brainstorming Session

Datasphere: Satellite transmitted data.

Debbie: A Baby Newbie.

Defrag: I need to relax.

Deep Linking: Linking to a page other than a site's homepage.

Deep Web = Invisible Web <-- Web sites that are not indexed by search engines.

Demo Monkey: Gives a really good demo.

Demo Scene = Rave Scene <-- an underground Carbon Community where the Elite Nerds show off their stuff.

Denizen = Baby Netizen

Destination Page: The page you intended to visit before you got sidetracked.

Destination Site = Portal.

Digital Jewelry: High-Tech devices that people wear.

Digital Kudzu: Small files placed in every hidey-hole on your computer during installations.

Digital Revolution: TEOTWAWKI because of Digital technology.

Digiterati = Digital + Lit**erati** of the Digital Revolution.

Digitizer: This person loves to convert hard copy <-- paper, pictures, etc. ---> into a Digital form.

Dirty Connection = Crummy Internet Connection

DoS Attack: Denial of **S**ervice **Attack** <-- an attack meant to disable a Network or computer.

Dot-Bomb = Bad Idea

Dot-Con: When **Con**ned by a **Dot**-Com site or while doing business on the Net.

Installing... B^)

Dot-Commers: People that work for a Dot-Com company or in the Net industry.

Dot-Commie: Someone who believes that everything on the Web should be FOC <-- also likes all things Dot-Com = -F2F IRL.

Dot's All Folks: RIP Dot-Com company.

Double Geeking: When a Geek uses two computers at the same time <-- +1 = Triple Geeking **B^)**

Downstream = Download Speed

Drump: A middle-aged pot-bellied intellectual shut-in that socializes only through the Net.

Drunk Mouse: I think it is kinda self explanatory <-- don't you think?

Dub-Dub-Dub = World Wide Web = 3XDub.

Dweeb: This species is considered Spod -1 and love to glorify themselves to try an impress you when they get a response to the question M or F. They never <-- and I mean Never! --> live up to the image they present. However, they can be the source of easy fodder for the seasoned Netizen.

E-Anything: The E stands for Electronic.

Ear Candy: Cool Sounds.

Easter Egg = Hidden Treasure = Fun Website

E-Collar Workers = Dot-Commers

Ego-Surfing: To perform a Net search on one's own name.

**Elancer = E + Free*lancer* = Geek who is plugged in and provides their services over the net.

Electron = Illogical Clicker

E-mail Shorthand = Geek Lingo

Emoticon = Attitude <-- like --> **8-]**

Encoding: The process of rewriting &/or transferring from one format to another.

End-User: You --> the person reading this book **:-)**

Eternal Hold: Placed on hold on the landline <-- Telephone --> for a very long time.

Event Horizon: A turning point in your life <-- becoming GLICS **;-)**

Evernet: The always-on, high-speed, broadband, ubiquitous multi-format Web.

Eye Candy = Cool graphics

Fat Binary = **Large Download**

Fat Finger: Oops when typing.

Fat Pipe = **High Capacity Wiring** = Super fast connection

Fire Off = **Send E-mail**

Flame: To send nasty or insulting personal attack messages rather than discuss opinions rationally.

Flame Bait: A posting that's deliberately inflammatory <-- an intent to elicit a strong reaction and start a flame war.

Flash crowd: Intense periods of heavy use on a network system.

Flavor: Full Flavor = Full Version --> Vanilla = Lite Version

Foo/Foobar: What's your Foo/Foobar ? <--What's your e-mail address?

Fram: Spam sent by family or friends.

Freenet: Go to the library :)

Freeware = **Free** Software

Frendor: A preFerred Vendor.

Frontdoor: The user interface for logging in to the Net, an App, or a Box.

Fudge Factor: A margin of error.

Gadget Fatigue: Gadget overloads resulting in possible Brain Fart.

Gamer: Expert @ playing E-Games.

Gatored: The act from a software plug-in that ambushes competitor sites with pop-ups triggered by keywords.

Gearhead: A Nerd or Geek obsessed with & has to have the latest Gadgets or Gizmos.

Geek = Nerd Newbie = Baby Nerd

Geek Lingo: A codified method of providing information <-- which of course --> can only be properly decoded by those that speak Geek.

Still Installing... B^)

Geeking Out: When you play computers while watching TV while talking on the Smart Phone while reading up on the latest technology and think that it is just to KEWL!

Geek Speak: Class of language that uses **G**eek **L**ingo **I**nternet and **C**ommunication **S**avvy vocabularies ;)

Geekosphere: Where Geeks show their colors IRL.

Geeksploitation: Taking advantage of Geeks.

Geektivist = **Geek** + **A**ctivist

Generation: Refers to the age of a Hacker
> * 1rst Generation: Born 1950 – 1969 One word Handles
> * 2nd Generation: Born 1970 -- 1989 Two word Handles
> * 3rd Generation: Born 1989 --> Use phrase Handles

Generation E = **Net Generation** <-- All Ages who are Netizens.

Genius Killer: Suppresses new technology.

Ghost Site: It tells you it's dead <-- Sometimes a useful Web site --> Sometimes a poltergeist!

Glitch: Unexpected interruption that can result in a crash <-- usually caused by a power surge or dirty connection <-- A Glitch is a hardware problem.

Gobbledygook: Incoherent strings of letters and symbols <-- Bad or encrypted data

Gonk: Your pulling my leg --> your **Gonk**ing me ;)

Googlewhacking: A game where a user types two words into the search line with the intent of trying to retrieve a single search result <-- if Results 1-1 of 1 appear You Win!

Gopher: Search engine for text-based/non-graphical sites.

Gopherhead: Someone obsessed with **Gopher** sites.

Graffiti: Handwriting recognition software <-- it can even recognize symbols that aren't letters!

Gremlins: Like Gobbledygook these mysterious characters sometimes <-- after a cut and paste --> will appear in text documents, code, or e-mail.

Grok: Do you get it? <-- Do you Grok?

Grrl = **Grrrl** = **Grrls** = **Grrlz** = **Female Netizen**

GUI: Graphical **U**ser **I**nterface <-- gooey --> what you see on your computer screen.

Gumint = Government

Hacker Jargon = Hacker Lingo

Hacktivist = Hacking + **Activism** = Electronic Civil Disobedience.

Hairball: A tangled mess <-- Bad code.

Handle = Screen Name

Handshake: When two modems agree on how to transfer data during a connection.

Handy = Cell Phone = Smart Phone

Hang Time = Computer Freeze

Hard Copy = P-mail = Printed document

Hijackware = Gatored = Scumware = Thiefware <-- Plug-in that Hijacks you and takes you to another Site.

Hive: Social life on the networks <-- a direct result of the digital revolution

Hollywired = Hollywood + **Wired** = Internet Media Products

Human Capital = Blood Supply = Living Assets = Employees

Hung: When the computer won't speak or the modem won't shut up.

I/O Error = Ignorant Operator Error

I-Anything: I = Internet

Iconoclast = Internet Consultant <-- they replace the traditional worker.

Illegal: Illegal operation error message <-- Don't worry --> your not in trouble --> your computer is.

In The Cloud: When learning the complexities of the net.

In The Pod: In an office cubical within an office cube farm.

Indie = Indy = Independent

Infotainment = Information + Enter**tainment**

Inmigrant: To leave the country to work as a Techie in another country.

Internaut = Trained Netizen

Internet Society: An organization that supports the Internet Evolution.

Internet Telephony = **Internet** - traditional **Telephone** + **Program** to transmit voice or fax = traditional Telephone - Long Distance Bill **;-)**

Intropreneur = **Intr**overted + Entre**preneur**

IP Address = Internet **P**rotocol **Address** = Internet + Street Address = Your Location on the Net <-- Everything logged in has one.

Ippie: 1rst in line for dedicated line no matter the $

Jabber: Meaningless chatter.

Jack In: To get connected.

Jaggies: Jagged edged images.

Kevork: To kill something.

Key Pal: An Internet Pen **Pal**.

Keyboard Trauma: Call a CERT <-- JK **:-)**

Kluge/Kludge = **Unattractive Solution** = Hacker trick to repair Bugs.

Koan: Riddle between Guru and Student <-- Kinda like this book. **B^)**

Lag/Lagging = Hang Time X <-- the X it takes U to go from **=8-O** to **:- "**

Lamer: Person who behaves stupidly.

Landing Page: Where U land after clicking a link.

Lingo: Unintelligible language that specializes in a particular field.

Link Farm: A site –good Content +++++++ links.

Linkrot: A Website with ++++++++ **Broken Links** suffers from this.

Llama = **Gamer - 1 + Lamer**

Looky-Loo: Internet + Window Shopping - Buying

Loser Error = **User** Error = Blames error on the computer = **Luser** Error

Luddite: Someone who violently opposes technology.

Lumpy: A Young 20-something Drump but will socialize IRL <-- usually at Sci-fi conventions.

Lurker: Visitor who hovers in a chat room without responding.

Getting There... |-O

Magic Smoke: If you see this coming out of your computer do this -->
=8-O <-- then call CERT. ATTENTION Newbies --> There is no
such thing as Magic Smoke stored in computer chips in order to make a
computer run! ;)

Malware = Malicious Software/Code

Mail Bomb: +1 Flame = Mail Server or Mail Reader Crash.

Martian Packet: X-file e-mails or strange data that show up
mysteriously.

Meatbot = You in the flesh.

MeatJail = Your Brain

Meatloaf: Homemade junk e-mail <-- ingredients usually consists of
jokes, trivia, stories etc...

MeatSpace = The Real World

Mecca = Mechanical

Metaverse = Virtual Reality

Microcontent: Brief summary <-- lists content, copyrights, thanx or
general info about a site.

MicroSerf = Baby Programmer

MicroSociety: A classroom society created by/for students for study.

Middle School Dance: The waiting before 2 systems integrate <-- both
are waiting for the other to initiate.

Modemhead: Net addict who believes the Net is Meatspace.

Mouse Potato = Modemhead – 1

Mousetrapping: An obnoxious trick to keep you captive on a site.

MUD: Multi-**U**ser **D**ungeon/**D**imension + simulation + creation <--
usually text-based.

Muggle = Baby Newbie <-- NO Net or computer experience.

Nar = Bad Vibes

Neologism = Baby Term

Neo-Luddite = Luddite – Violence

Nerd: A brainy person that knows everything <-- and I mean
everything! --> there is to know about the Internet and Computers.

Net Head = Web Head = Modem Head - 1 <-- someone who is passionate about the internet.

Net Lag = Net Delay <-- 2 many CyberTourists or a Dirty Connection.

Net Personality: Known to 1000's on the Net.

Net Police = Moral Police <-- Remember your Netiquette!

Net.God: From the beginning <-- of the Net --> They Know All and have Done All **0|-)**

Netary Public: Provides digital copyright protection via a Cybertrail.

Netcentric: Company that entails the Net and its technologies to further its business initiatives.

Netiquette: Must we go through all that again?

Netizen = Experienced Cytizen = Baby Geek

NetSplit = Loss of Contact

Netsploitation = Net + Exploitation

Network Pirate = Coworker Jerk who harasses through company's LAN.

Newbie = Newborn Cytizen = Baby Denizen

Nonlinear Behavior: Erratically Flaming = Overemotional Idiot

Not Found 404: Return error message given when trying to locate a site --> the requested URL was not found on this server.

NSA Line Eater: National **S**ecurity **A**gency <-- **Beware** Gumint could be reading **;)**

Nym = Handle = Screen Name = Pseudo**Nym**

Off The Grid = Creativity = Independence from the normal system.

Ohnosecond: The split second before **=8-O**

On Velvet = Sitting Pretty

Online Jargon: I think we've been through this --> remember Geek Lingo **;)**

Otaku = Avid Collecters

Over-Mac'd: Over simplifying.

Packet = DataGrams <-- info pieces/data units sent over the Net.

PacketSpace: The **Air** Packets are sent through to a Handy.

Pain In The Net = **Flamer**

PageJacking: Stealing a Web page to use on your own site.

Parasite: A site that frames another site <-- making it seem like their own content.

Patch = **Digital Duct Tape** <-- fixes software problems.

Penguinhead = **Open Source Linux Geeks**

Peripheralitis: 2 many **Peripherals** X 0 plugins = no communication.

Pervasive Computing: To Webify society by flooding it with easy access to digital data.

Phreak: Hacks the phone company.

PimpWare = **Freeware Fake** <-- part of a bigger marketing scheme.

Pin Bender = **Shoddy Techie**

PING: Packet **IN**ternet **G**roper <-- a protocol for testing an IP address' accessibility by sending a packet to it and waiting for a reply.

Pirate: Person who commits digital piracy.

Pixel Pusher: Person who makes changes to images 4 $

Playground = **Techie Workspace** = **Sandbox**

Plonk = **Kill** + **Persons Message**

Plugged-in = **Connected** = **Jack In** = **Wired**

P-Mail = **Tree Mail** = **Snail Mail** = **Printed Mail**

PoachWare = **ThiefWare** <--Software that Steals digital property.

Pomo = **PostModern**

Ponytails: Art directors/Creative Professionals.

PostMaster: Master of a Newsgroup <-- person to complain to/ask ?'s.

Prairie Dogging: The cause for everyone's heads to pop up in a cube farm.

Prolly = **Probably**

Propeller Head = **Plastic Pocket-Protector Set** = **Old-Fashioned Nerds**

Props: Compliments and Thanx <-- Special Props to U for opening this book! **B^)**

Prosumer: Software Purchaser for **Pro**fessional + **Con**sumer reasons.

PurePlay = **Clicks**-&-Mortar **– Mortar** <-- sells Only over the Net.

Puter = Com**Puter Illiterate**

Queue = **Waiting Area**

Quick-&-Dirty = **Kludge**

QWERTY = Keyboard <-- IC 1rst 6 letters in upper left row.

Rain Fade: The loss of a satellite signal due to heavy rainfall.

Ramp Up = **Getting Psyched**

Rasterbator = **Compulsive Pixel Pusher**

Raw Click: Exact Click count.

Return Code: A Server Message you might see when surfing <-- reports the Return status of a Web page.

Reverse Engineering = **Decoding Code**

Rib Site: Regional Service directly connected to the Backbone.

Ringmaster: Master of a Web**Ring**.

Road Warrior: They travel frequently for their job.

Rogue Site: A malicious Web site that gives you many headaches.

RollerBall = **Mouse** + Track**Ball**

Scenerio Net: A group of sites brought together to provide tools to complete a **Scenario** like --> purchasing a car or taking a vacation <-- all services are accessible through these networks to accomplish the many tasks involved

Schadenfreude: Schaden = Damage + **Freude** = Joy <-- the **Joy** one feels for the **Damage** to others.

Scooby Snacks: No $ Rewards.

Screenagers = **Connected Teenagers**

Screen Name: The name U go by in a chat room

Screen-saver Face: The look a person gets on their face during a Brain Fart.

Script kiddies: A Netizen who locates tools to attack other Netizens or Net systems.

Shareware: Try it B4 U buy it.

Shareware Girl/Boy = **Office Tramp**

Sheeple = Sheep + Peo**Ple** <-- obediently follow all the fads and trends.

ShelfWare = CoasterWare = Worthless Software

Shipper = Fan Fiction Writer = Relation**Shipper** <-- fantasizes about romantic relationships between characters and then writes about it.

Shopping Bot: Bot that does the comparison **Shopping** 4U.

Shortys: If I recall I think we went through this. **;)**

SHOUTING: When you keep your CAPS LOCK ON LIKE THIS IT IMPLIES THAT I AM YELLING AT YOU TO MAKE MY POINT!

Signal 2 Noise Ratio: Measurement of useful information.

Siliconia = High-Tech Geographical Nicknames <-- relates to cities/areas that are swimming in high-tech businesses.

Singing Daisy: The final action B4 the computer died --> permanently.

Skeet = Obsolete Handy

Skitzo: Different Handles + 1 or more used in a chat room at the same time.

Slinging Code: When a Programmer is on a roll.

Smart Phone = Digital phone = PDA = any Handy that's integrated with a data service.

Smurf: Hacker who DoS Attacks by flinging PING.

Sneakernet: To join this crowd --> copy a floppy then walk it to the recipient.

Sniffer: Snooping Software that steals and spreads passwords or eavesdrops.

Snippet: Small piece of Info.

Soft Copy = E-mail = Electronic Document

Spam = Junk E-mail = **S**tupid **P**ersons **A**dvertise**M**ent = UCA

Spew: Jabber over and over and over and over and over and over and over.

Spider = Crawler

Splash Page: The 1rst fancy introductory page on a site that leads U to the main site <-- usually shows cool stuff like animations or videos.

Almost There... 8-)

Spod: This low life form likes to annoy Talkers and MUDs. Typically has few friends IRL where they have a failure of communication. Geek -1 without any true <3 for computers they lack in knowledge/interest of networks and believe that access is a their given right <-- then they clog lines in order to reach new Talkers or MUDS --> follow passed on instructions on how to sneak in <-- then complain about busy routes! Like Dweebs they start off with M or F? <-- but then ask for numbers IDs and passwords <-- and thus their stupid circle starts again -->.

Spoofing: When a Smurf fakes its location during a DoS Attack.

SpyWare: Software that tracks surfing habits.

Sticky Content: Content that makes U **Stick**/return to a site.

Subs = **Sub**scribers

Squidzillionaire: Make way to much $ for what they do.

Swiped Out: Credit card that no longer works.

Synthespian = **Syn**thetic + **Thespian** = Electronic Actor <-- human form that dwells in a 3D VR.

SYSOP = **SYS**tem **OP**erator <-- maintains a BBS

Talk or Talker: Unless you know the special codes don't bother knocking on this technology <-- it is generally reserved for Programmers, Sysops & advanced Techies

Tchotchkes = Promotional Knickknacks

Techie: Certified Geek specializing in the hardware and software in computers.

Techies Day = October 2nd

Technobabble: Technical jargon strung together to sound impressive <-- without really meaning anything to technical--> usually used to overwhelm Denizens.

Technojunkie: Gear Head who suffers from Gadget Fatigue & Upgrade Fever because of fetish for hardware.

Technophile: Elder **Techno**logy supporter who surfaced during the 1970's.

Telco = **Tel**ecommunications **Co**mpany = TPC

Telematics: Telecommunication + Computers + Vehicle Function = Smart Cars!

Tennis E-mail: Meaningless e-mail sent back and forth.

Text M8 = E-mail Pal = Chat Pal <-- Your Friends!

Text Me = IM Me = Call Me <-- via Text/Instant messaging

The End: Ever think you'll reach it? --> Me neither <-- Wait! --> I meant the last page on the Net!

The Real World = Carbon Community = MeatSpace <-- the space You are currently inhabiting in the flesh.

Think Time: The idle **Time** during a long download to actually **Think**!

Three Big C's = 3BCs = Content **+ C**ommunity **+ C**ommerce

Three Deadly Middles = 3DeadMids = Middle + Aged/Class/Management

Throttling: Connection Speed Restriction <-- I can't drive 55 **B^"**

Thumb-Typing: Typing with Thumbs **;-a** <-- seriously --> usually done on Smart Phones.

Topic Drift: Playing Tennis E-mail with a false subject matter header.

Tradigital = Tradition + **Digital =** Digital culture passed down from generation 2 generation.

Treeware = Paper-Based Print

Triority: Three top priorities.

Troll: Uses Flame Bait for tricks and giggles.

Tron: To become inaccessible except through IM or e-mail.

Turklebaum = Phony Rumors = Bogus Content on the Net = Misinformation

Tweak: To make Bigger Faster Stronger.

Unknown Zone: The space U R traveling B4 reaching the next site.

Unplugged = Not Connected

Upgrade Fever: Obsessed with Upgrading.

Upstream = Upload Speed

Username: The name you use to access the Net or other important programs <-- usually a part of your e-mail address. 4 Xtra security --> keep Username and Screen Name different.

Vanity Page = Personal Website

VaporWare = WonderWare <-- Hyped software nowhere 2B found.

Velveeta = ECP

Virus: Program that replicates and infects through shared Programs.

Vortals = Vertical **Portals** <-- caters to a specific industry.

VR = Virtual Reality = **3D World**

Vulcan Nerve Pinch = Three Finger Salute = Quadruple Bucky example --> soft boot using ACD.

Walled garden: When an ISP gives easier access to its own <-- or paid for --> Content.

Wankware = X-rated software

WAP = **W**ireless **A**pplication **P**rotocol <-- gives Smart Phone secure access to the Net.

Wapplet = **WAP** + **A**pplet <-- content for a Smart Phone

Web Bug = Cookie Cousin <-- Tiny image tags buried in source code that tell Merchants your IP Address and what things you have <-- or have not --> responded to.

Web Graffiti: A technology that allows a user to paste Stinky Notes all over a Web site.

Web Guide = Search Engine

Web Guru = Webmaster +1 <-- They develop the best and coolest sites out there.

Web Head: Advanced Netizen who truly **<3** the Web!

Web Hippie = Netizen + Culture + Freedom of Information/Expression = **0|-)**

Webcentric: Any Idea that entails the web.

Webify = Webification <-- to convert anything from its original format into useful Web format.

WebRing: Shared theme sites linked together.

Websmith = Webmaster <-- Designer/Developer of Web Sites

Webster = Denizen

Webtop: Desktop that's accessed remotely through the Web.

Wetware = MeatJail

Wire Jam = Slow Internet Connection

Worder: Considers the Puter a glorified typewriter.

Word-of-mouse: Gossip by e-mail.

Worm = **W**rite **O**nce **R**ead **M**any = **Virus**

Yetties = **Y**oung **E**ntrepreneurial **T**wenty-something **Techies** = Yuppie + Techie

Yoyo mode: Computer go up <-- Fast --> Computer go down.

Zine = Electronic Maga**Zine**

Zipperhead = **Closed Mind**

Zombie: A dead Web site that remains alive.

Installation Complete!
Congrats
Q:-)

Read Me

;)

Trouble Shooting:

If your eyes become crossed <-- uncross them or --> make sure your glasses are on correctly and you have kept all drinks at bay!

For any kinks in the neck go into Chinese/Japanese mode <-- or if worst comes to worst --> See your chiropractor!

If you become bored --> Get A Life!

Close this book, take a deep breath <-- maybe go to the bathroom, maybe get a drink --> and start again.

Technical Support:

Go to --> www.glics.com

Or --> www.lulu.com/glics

As always --> stay wired and look for patches and upgrades.

Props & Scooby Snacks:

OM   <-- U Keep me grounded and on track <-- even though IDASAD W/ U and <3 U wayyyyyy 2 much ;)

DD <-- My sweet little mini me Boo ;) **XOXOXO** I <3 U w/all my soul

DB <-- No questions asked & I <3 U 4 it

Bang! You found an Easter Egg |

V

----------> IDASAD

I Dream **A**bout **S**ex **A**ll **D**ay

Encode and then Upload <-- maybe <-- just
maybe --> you can teach me a thing or 2
BCNU ;)

<-- | White Space <-- use it...
V